Leading up to retirement, Arthur Gardner had many conversations with a close friend about what they would do. When it finally came to "What now?" the friend retorted, "For a start, there's your life story: war time evacuation, failed the 11 plus, 5-year apprenticeship, 2 years National Service, marriage, children, work, lifestyle change, the awful retirement experience and much, much more."

That spurred Arthur on to write over 70,000 words about the different stages of his life. At the age of 26, he changed careers; reading the *Daily Mirror* one day, the *Telegraph* the next. After many years in commerce, finally Arthur, leading up to retirement, spent some years as a self-employed landscape gardener. Leaning on his own experiences, in parallel with scripting his life story, Arthur has also penned this account of life in a fictitious retirement property.

The characters and events in this book are fictitious. Any apparent similarity to real persons is not intended by the author and is either a coincidence or the product of your own troubled imagination.

Arthur Gardner

BLOOMING
SPOILSPORTS

AUSTIN MACAULEY PUBLISHERS™

LONDON • CAMBRIDGE • NEW YORK • SHARJAH

A CIP catalogue record for this title is available from the British Library.

ISBN 9781786126535 (Paperback)
ISBN 9781786126542 (Hardback)
ISBN 9781786126559 (E-Book)
www.austinmacauley.com

First Published (2017)
Austin Macauley Publishers Ltd.
25 Canada Square
Canary Wharf
London
E14 5LQ

Dedication

I dedicate my story to the many other mature citizens who have encountered similar experiences. There is life after retirement, be positive and constructive, it helps and that I have proved. The truth will always come out in the end.

To my loyal wife, whose help and support enable us to become much stronger symbionts and, of course, our long-suffering family and empathising friends.

2018.

RICHARD 2 CAROLINE.

My First Book.

ENSoy!

Chapter 1

Here we are at Orton Villas, formerly The Old Vicarage, North Cornwall. My name is Sam and this story is about me and my wife, Lily, and our personal experiences residing in a very well-known, publicly acclaimed retirement home for the over 55-year-olds.

The story begins in the autumn of 2007. Sam and Lily had prematurely lost their respective partners in 1992. Sam's dear Beatrice, aged 57, and a lovely, caring father in Francis, aged 52. Five years later, Sam and Lily married and after a day's honeymoon in Naples, settled down to married life.

Sam was 62 and Lily 51, they had six children between them, none of whom were living at home.

From the beginning of their marriage, they lived in Sam's house in a small town in Cornwall. Sam had lived in the town since 1986, Lily joined him in 1997; a lovely location, not a village, but a town of around 2,000 residents. This would be where, from their back garden, they would run their landscape and flower bedding business. To support that enterprise, Sam was also able to rent a large wooden-structured greenhouse a short distance away.

An important aspect of this business was that for 20 years, Sam had a stall at the local town fair, also called a street market. He was extremely successful at that. Overall, the flower side, preparing, growing and planting their stock—both in summer and autumn—was a large part of Sam's business.

In 2008, they left their house behind to embark on a new venture. They moved into an old vicarage in a nearby large town, specifically converted into retirement accommodation and rebranded as Orton Villas. This came with an enormous garden, much bigger than the average size for a retirement complex. In the first three years, this proved a delight for many residents, culminating in numerous gardening awards over that time, including one from the Royal Horticultural Society. Soon, the landlord, Sunshine Homes' management, became aware that they were not getting the plaudits themselves, the residents were. So, taking umbrage to the receipt of the awards, they sought to extinguish the delight of the residents, claiming that they did not want a show garden.

How did it come to that? Why did Sunshine Homes get to the point where they were so unhappy with the residents managing the gardens of their home? To understand that we need to look at the story of the disappointment of Bradley and Olga's management; one official, one unofficial, and of how they chose to run Orton Villas. Bradley and Olga were in place as caretakers, representing Sunshine Homes' management. They received a two-bedroom accommodation facility onsite, rent-free plus a free parking space solely for their personal use.

In September 2007, Sam and Lily had decided on a change of lifestyle. They found Orton Villas through a local newspaper advert and saw it as a great way to move gracefully into retirement. In spring 2008, they moved very excitedly into a one-bedroom flat. Like others, they chose a southeast-facing balcony, which would allow a sunny location nearly all day. This also gave a good outlook over the lovely gardens.

Their decision to locate here was based on all the wonderful information presented to them by the Sunshine Homes sales woman. How much of that was genuine?

They met Sandra, the initial caretaker, on their arrival at Orton Villas; she greeted them very warmly and proved to be a very supportive person. Sadly, Sandra died a few months later of cancer and that was the moment for Bradley and Olga to move into Orton Villas. Olga, at 60, was already entrenched as caretaker in another retirement accommodation nearby but only part-time. Bradley, at 66, left his previous establishment, a much older retirement complex, seeing the new Orton Villas development as an opportunity for him to initially become caretaker, with Olga, being much younger, in the wings to succeed him. He was rubbing his hands with glee but didn't perhaps realise how lucky he really was—a brand-new building, new management, new residents and a completely new start. All this was a perfect opportunity for Bradley and Olga to manage Orton Villas how they wanted to, not necessarily in the best interests of the residents, whose home they were about to be living in.

Soon after Bradley and Olga arrived, a social committee was formed; Joe was elected chairman, Olga secretary, Jean treasurer, and finally, Sam and Julie were added. The committee's function was to arrange social events, such as fish and chip suppers, bingo and quizzes. For each event, the committee not only prepared but also cleared up every item as a rule and it really began to work well.

Joe's experience was originally very much approved of. He was a strong character, with many years of voluntary work and this showed. The committee had to be run 'proper'. Although Bradley was caretaker, Olga was not very happy. From early on, she did not like the fact that she was not in control, but more of that later. Slowly, it was working well, functions were ticking along, and in those early days, as many as 25 residents attended each function. This was very good, given that some of the total 40 flats had not been sold.

The ladies in the flats preferred to make food for the functions—items like sausage rolls, a lovely cheese board, salmon plate, beautiful assorted sandwiches, special pork sausages—rather than buy. This highlighted the class of residents. So, the residents were bonding well. Life at Orton Villas was turning out as Sam and Lily had expected: coffee mornings on Monday and Friday, Bradley chatting in a friendly way, Sam always having a joke over his favourite biscuits, everything was going well; on the surface, at least.

Chapter 2

After only a few weeks of opening, there was an incident which would have a large effect on the 20 or so residents having already moved in. It was about the car park at the rear of the main building.

When all residents moved in, there would only ever be enough car spaces for 16 cars. Sunshine Homes argued that although there were 40 flats, as time passed, only 16 spaces would be needed. They assumed residents would gradually give their cars up. That was the theory anyway.

One early occupier called Barbara, dreadfully disabled, had especially bought a two-bedroom flat on the ground floor for the obvious reasons relating to her disability. Up until early June 2008, no one had mentioned that parking was actually 'first come, first served', least of all the sales staff.

Eventually, it came to pass that Barbara was not able to park her car in the main rear car park due to a lack of space. There were only nine such 2-bed flats as Barbara's, all at premium prices, with the remaining 1-bed flats all significantly cheaper. It soon became obvious that car spaces would be at a premium; most times Barbara found a space, she always hoped it would be close to her flat for ease of access. Some residents were sympathetic and helpful, some were not so. Here's the story.

On this particular occasion, Barbara came home and found the car park full. This was always a possibility, which would mean if available, one would have to park in the five-space visitors' car park at the front. So here is the picture. Naturally, first come first served is the situation, but Barbara being very disabled, was unable to walk the distance to/from the front car park, even with a stick.

Understandably, concerned for her access and believing she was entitled to a parking space 'out-back', Barbara fired her anger firstly at Bradley, the caretaker. His reply was, "This is how it is. There is nothing I can do."

Now, really fired up, Barbara headed straight for the sales office, which was still on-site as a number of flats remained vacant. She confronted Liz, the sales manager, shouting excitedly, "I have spent £250,000 plus at Orton Villas and I do not have the car space I was led to believe I was entitled to." Liz, stunned by Barbara's sudden entry into the office and subsequent demanding outburst, started to get emotional.

During the confrontation, the office door flew open and standing there were Joe, the social committee chairman, and Olive, another resident. Olive was waving a petition, prepared earlier by various residents against the attitude that was being adopted by Barbara. It was suggesting that they should get rid of Barbara. By now, Liz was lying on a settee, crying and clearly in some distress.

Joe and Olive started remonstrating with Barbara, "Who do you think you are?"

Barbara replied strongly, "I was told there would always be a car park space for me. Where is it?" By now, with Liz more settled and comforted, Joe and Olive were also composed but not before reminding Barbara that her outburst was out of order. She replied, "This is not over. You will see!" Everything had shown what a problem parking at Orton Villas was going to become.

All the confrontation did was to draw attention to the existing problem. This resulted in at least 12 residents immediately showing their resentment towards Barbara's attitude. Sadly, it was never to go away.

Sunshine Homes' management never showed serious concern about the car park problem. This would become a bigger problem for all residents in time, those to whom the residents paid their dues being unsympathetic to their cause whilst their employees, Bradley and Olga, continued to enjoy free accommodation, free car parking and many other benefits.

Yes, it was a bad start and things were only going to get worse. Apart from that unfortunate incident, Sam, Lily and their fellow residents were all settling in well. Christmas 2008 came around quickly and many of the residents celebrated their first Yuletide at Orton Villas, with a brass band courtesy of Joe, a large decorated Christmas tree and much shared revelry. There was also a well-supported first Christmas Carol event. In a further attempt to be seen as inclusive, Bradley and Olga joined in with the festivities.

So, 2009 came in. By early spring, it was clear that Sunshine Homes had contracted a gardener to manage the grounds. Rod was his name, and he had a mate who had the unenviable task of managing the vast lawns. This is when Sam asked Bradley, "Can Lily and I work in the garden?"

He replied, "I don't see why not. Olga and I enjoy doing that; in fact, Olga is very experienced and very knowledgeable."

"Good," Sam said, "so are many of the able-bodied residents." It set Sam thinking, especially just moving into his retirement after 20 plus years' experience in the gardening business. The outlook was good, or was it?

Chapter 3

Now Sam's shared dream was working fast. He had approval to work in the gardens, so how was it going to work? A few months before, Sam had acquired an allotment and this was to prove very successful in growing vegetables and now, flowers. There was a greenhouse in situ, a contribution for it was given to the previous allotment holder. This would be useful for growing flower seeds and plants for the Orton Villas' gardens at very little cost.

Sam's contacts were still in the area for the wholesale provision of plants, compost and fertilisers. What was now needed: quantities of flowers, the cost, and where will funds come from? Well, fortunately, Sam had all the answers; remember, for 20 years, this had been Lily and Sam's way of life. Funding would be sought from voluntary contributions from residents.

Previously, one of their normal tasks each year was to create a calendar plan for planting gardens. So, Sam and Lily adopted this approach for Orton Villas. Their plan would commence in January, running till the end of May. Linking up with the local 'In Bloom' annual garden competition in the local town, the residents found that Orton Villas would be placed in a newly created community class.

A meeting of the residents was approved by Bradley, and no doubt Olga naturally too, albeit Sam could not understand why such a meeting required the caretakers' approval. Many residents attended, some offering a variety of options to support the growth of 'their' gardens, some with cash, all logged properly by Sam in a special book. During that meeting, it was agreed that Sam would send an entry into the local gardening competition on behalf of the residents of Orton Villas.

Plans for the gardens were agreed upon by 98% of residents and this focussed on only growing summer bedding plants.

Twenty areas of the huge garden were chosen as sites, with all the details left to Sam and Lily to manage on behalf of the residents.

Some residents, notably Sid and Olive, were not interested in bedding plants. It was their wish to create their own plan for a self-funded area of other plants, not bedding plants, adjacent to the rear car park. That was agreeable to the other residents, so Sid and Olive, along with Sam and Lily, collected the structural elements for that garden. To their credit, they were able to assemble these into a well-presented garden, including the not-insignificant manual labour required. Sam, who was well into the garden by now, just felt that this subtle split with Sid and Olive would grow. In time, this split would widen, as this story will sadly show.

Now then! It was all very well planning a flower garden, but who was the gardener?

Well, Rod had been working at Orton Villas for Sunshine Homes for a year now and was coping well;

he trimmed everywhere and kept the garden looking neat. Most importantly, he also had a good rapport with most of the residents, including Lily and Sam. His helper quietly mowed all the grass areas too. Rod also worked, albeit cautiously, alongside Bradley. They clashed now and again, but Rod was the consummate professional at all times.

The residents were allowed to help in the garden, deadheading plants and carrying out other general maintenance within their capabilities, even the occasional weeding, but Rod was always considered to be the gardener. The bedding plants were all growing well in Sam's greenhouse in readiness for the displays in the coming summer. They ranged from geraniums, through bedding begonias to lovely cosmos, various sizes of sunflowers and many more varieties.

In early May, all the daffodils planted by Sam and Lily the previous autumn, with agreement from Bradley, had grown fully. They would be left uncut until early June. However, Rod was expecting all spring flowers, wallflowers, tulips, etc. to usually be cleared by late May. Acquiescing with that, Sam and Lily agreed that Rod would dispose of the spring flowers by early June, allowing them to progress— with the other residents—towards planting of the new bedding stock. Sam and Lily were overwhelmed with the offers of help from other enthusiastic residents. Some of them were less able than others and they did not have the appropriate tools either, so Sam and Lily provided the tools and also placed the trays of plants ready for their willing helpers.

Come early June in the very first year, all flowers were ready for planting; well-watered, all done under the watchful eye of Bradley. After all, water costs money, albeit not his money.

Although Sam and Lily had the support of about 16 residents, some were a little sceptical of how it would really work. For a first effort, the financial support was magnificent, so they were at last ready to go. Sam reminded everyone that all the plants were half the retail price simply because they were self-grown from seeds in his greenhouse. There were red geraniums all over, multi-coloured bedding begonias, beautiful 12-inch sunflowers with fantastic deep-yellow colours, placed in a prominent border, even a few giant ones were planted.

Once the collective effort of planting had been completed, it just left the final task of watering all the flowers in; in fact, puddling them in is the best way. Again, Bradley was watching like a hawk over how much of 'their' water the residents were using. So, after a busy day—having been served plenty of cups of tea, the odd one laced with brandy, loads of home-made cakes, plenty of enthusiasm and most importantly, every one showing a sense of purpose—the residents considered it a job well done.

So, next was the visit in July from the 'In Bloom' judges, then the long wait for their decision in mid-August. The beautiful, large garden came alive; residents really saw this and responded with much enthusiasm. Then, around mid-August, a personal letter arrived from the chairperson of the local garden competition, called the Town's Best In Bloom Competition. On opening it, there was the result: second in the Community Award. Sam, along with Bradley, was invited with two or three other residents to attend the local rugby club for the presentation. This was held in the early evening one day in September.

Only Bradley came with Sam to a room full of many present, with a bar as well as a lovely 'spread'. Bradley seemed to know every one present; Sam presumed that would be down to his local charity connections.

So, the presentation opened, and as the evening progressed, the excitement grew. Many winners were first timers, some as ever old hands. Then suddenly, Orton Villas' name was called in second place for the community section. Both Bradley and Sam were well pleased. Of course, on their arrival back to Orton Villas, all was quiet; well, it was after 9 pm. It is of note that many winners remained behind. As it happened every year, a special cup was presented to a local resident, who displayed the Best Overall Garden in the judge's opinion. Imagine that! The best garden in our local town, knowing 40,000 people live there.

Chapter 4

After all this unexpected garden success, Orton Villas' residents wanted more.

So by now, with the garden a blooming success, residents began to ask if they could have a plan for autumn planting of spring flowers like daffodils, tulips and wallflowers etc. This would be easy for Sam and Lily to organise if financed as before by residents' contributions and planting, and also with help, as before, from volunteer residents. Of course, this was with the full consent of Bradley (and Olga) and Rod, the gardener.

So, come late October, summer beds and borders were emptied and planting began with full support of everyone for the following spring.

So, into the new year, the committee meetings continued, with Sam in regular attendance. They were good, many events were planned. However, two observant committee members were noticing that when dates for events were discussed, Olga would return to her flat for her diary to establish availability of dates and whether she and Bradley would be available to attend. It was debated why it mattered if the caretaker and his wife were busy on that particular date, after all, these were social events for residents. It always transpired that Olga won out and the dates were tongue in cheek agreed to coincide with free dates on her calendar. Some members thought that occasionally, it would be nice to run events for themselves. This never seemed to happen.

Unbeknown to many residents, Bradley and Olga were able to claim time back when attending such 'social' events. Was this ethical? Sam and Lily (and some other residents) saw this as the very first signs of Bradley and Olga seeking to assert a level of control over the residents in their own homes. In their defence, however, Sam was not prepared to rock the boat too much as Bradley continued to allow residents permission to plan the garden and physically assist.

Events on a day-to-day basis continued, with Bradley being extremely particular in all his maintenance work. Some residents questioned if he had some form of obsessive compulsive disorder. There were no complaints in general, in fact, mostly praise, but there were always occasions when he would interfere in a project to save money and would fail. Sam saw gardening knowledge as one of these failings, and Bradley certainly was not very practical in general. His lack of expertise cost Orton Villas dearly. Final comment here is that his household husbandry could not be faulted, but his interference showed a lack of true management skills, which you either have or don't. Bradley had none. Many residents saw daily evidence of Bradley's primary function being to save money, rather than support them in 'their' home. Sam questioned if there was an annual bonus incentive for caretakers? He thought there certainly must be.

Then there was Barbara, yes nearly every day, she would have some outcry regarding parking. Remember, Orton Villas was still taking in new residents with fewer spaces; at times, there were many more cars than spaces available. Sunshine Homes even offered a one-off bounty to entice drivers to relinquish their vehicles. Why should they? Just because of short sightedness from Sunshine Homes? Bradley regularly defended his management company with comments like, "There is nothing I can do to help." He was lucky he had his own designated space, yet some disabled residents like Barbara's comments were continually falling on stony ground.

Still, life carried on at Orton Villas. There was still a postman and the milkman came three times a week. Rod the gardener was becoming increasingly frustrated by Bradley's interference in running the garden. This was being picked up by one or two residents. One example would show Rod having a professional plan, then Bradley suggesting an alternative, usually an out-of-season one and as Bradley saw himself as 'the boss', this was very frustrating for Rod. In time, Rod would leave Orton Villas, following many such disagreements over the garden.

Subsequently, Bradley would hire a man called Clive as the gardener. Clive was a local Mr Fix-It with whom Bradley was friends, certainly no gardener.

The annual garden plan was agreed upon for another year way back in January and was coming along nicely. After the first house meeting, Sam was very pleased as everything was dropping into place as June approached.

Chapter 5

So here we are, as ever, all the spring plants were cleared in late May, ready for the summer planting. The summer stock was in situ, having been grown by Sam in his greenhouse. The sun had its hat on and the band of happy volunteer residents was raring to go.

This year, as many as 21 residents would be available to assist planting during the day. There were tea ladies busy in the kitchen, ladies with disability trollies carrying homemade cakes, residents with hand forks, hand trowels, kneelers, etc.

Among the others, very noticeable were two residents—a husband and wife team—deadheading, sitting at one of two lovely garden seats, which they personally purchased for Orton Villas a few months earlier. They were preparing in a very methodical way for daffodil and tulip bulbs to be saved for the next season. This couple was noticeable not only for their enthusiastic endeavours, but also the fact that one of them had recently been diagnosed with the onset of dementia and was improving remarkably due to his gardening experience.

Elsewhere, both Sam and Lily were busy placing the plants. Like ants, many residents were well stuck into planting the plants as placed. There was a hive of activity, many smiley faces and a real community spirit. The plants were very varied as in the previous year: assorted geraniums—pinks, reds, salmon, apple blossom and even the odd white ones; colourful reds; whites of bedding begonias; even small bedding sunflowers; and many more varieties.

Watching all this activity, happiness and job satisfaction, Sam remembered looking on with Lily and whispering, "This could be Orton Villas' time in the annual completion."

"We will wait and see," she replied cautiously.

As ever, the final task was watering in the plants. The best way as before was to puddle them in. This was carried out by Bradley, very aware not to overdo it as he used the hosepipe. Sam pondered to himself if the water bill got paid out of Bradley's pocket?

On this planting day in early June, just like the planting plan was being carried out, there was also activity in laying a section of new lawn. This involved Bradley, Olga and also invited was Clive, the new gardener that Sam and Lily believed was in Bradley's pocket. This section of new lawn stemmed from the need to revise the layout of the front car park. Back in January, 18 months from the development opening, an agreement was reached by Sunshine Homes, to have some ruined plastic car park surfacing replaced. It was established by residents that it was not fit for purpose.

There would be no charge for this expensive work of getting the plastic removed, at a considerable cost saving. However, residents saw the benefit of replacing an area with new turf. To allow this to happen, funds were needed to pay for the turf and labour for laying it. Fortunately, a resident who overlooked this area of the garden/car park was happy to pay the cost to vastly improve her outlook. So, on this day in June, Sam, Lily and their fellow residents were planting for their second consecutive entry into the town's gardening competition whilst side by side was the Sunshine Homes turf-laying team.

Whilst the planting was going really well, all was not rosy with the turf laying.

Bradley was suggesting how he was going to effect his turf-laying plan. Previously, the ground had allegedly been prepared and Sam, even with his wealth of professional knowledge and experience, had made every effort to keep his distance. After all, Bradley was in charge. However, Olga arrived on the scene and started to direct the turf laying with no prior knowledge or experience.

Sam could see from his standpoint across the garden that Olga's involvement was only making things worse, so he offered his professional expertise. Not prepared to accept this help, an argument developed over how the work should be done; Sam decided to disappear as it was becoming nasty. He hurried back to the security of his flat. Hot on his heels came Bradley, huffing and puffing and shouting abuse. With his foot almost in the door, Bradley yelled, "I want an apology from you, Olga is very upset over your comments and attitude over the lawn work."

Stunned, Sam, for his peace of mind, reluctantly agreed. He commented that it was another attempt by Bradley to dig his heels in, despite his total inability to fully understand the correct procedure with this project, and once again, needing to show his authority. So now he, Bradley, was back in full control.

Bradley continued with the lawn, a project which—Sam knew from what he was seeing—would prove to be a total disaster in the long term. The preparation of the site was awful. Turf laying was a job for someone with experience; this was the occasion when Bradley would fail. He was stubborn, he knew it all. Later that week, the area manager Helga, on seeing the results would naturally take Bradley's side and confirm that the project was fit for its purpose.

Olga and Bradley then used the oscillator to keep the turf well-watered. No worry about cost here then, but then it was their decision, not the house's. After all, it was someone else's money, not theirs. The house was aware of the importance of cost when using water, so it would be important at this stage to be careful and not over indulge, but it was very necessary at the same time.

To draw this project to a close, as the organiser of the project, Clive (Mr Fix-It) went to take around the account to our benefactor widow, who knew a little about gardening. The labour cost was £175 (no doubt he shared the proceeds with Bradley). She argued that it was not fit for purpose. "Nothing to do with me. See Bradley, he is the manager." She did so later, but to no avail.

Then he retorted, "We can't use too much water. It will recover, it will be fine." Remember readers, it is June! All true gardeners know that it is very important to make sure that the turf gets well-watered in so that it can establish itself.

The resident paid a further £180 for the turf, the total cost came to £675. Time would show how the work turned out to be wrongly carried out and would remain so forever. Now six years on, spring reveals the ugly brown patch of lawn. This saddens this lovely gardening widow, who rightly describes all them of them as 'cowboys'. Later, we shall hear of other work which had resulted in a disaster.

So as summer developed, the displays were looking superb. The new lawn was not taking well, but then Sam was aware of this.

Soon, July would arrive, this is when the local judges would be visiting the large garden. Talking to them was not allowed, but they knew that two of them would visit and the residents would know who they were because they would be carrying clipboards. In the meantime, lots of weeding and deadheading was taking place. Occasionally, residents would also need to water some plants; this they did discretely. The weather, well, it had also been generally good.

Then suddenly, without any official warning, a car turned up, a lady and a gentleman got out, both holding clipboards. Sam received a phone call and on the other end was Barbara. "They are here," she said excitedly.

So this was the day the residents had been waiting for. The judges stayed about 45 minutes. Now, all they could do was to wait until late August for a result.

Chapter 6

Sam and Lily were due to travel to see family overseas at the end of the summer.

Luckily, Sam telephoned the local Bloom Garden secretary and because of their holiday, asked if the results of the competition were in. "They came in this morning," she replied, "but I can at this time answer just one question for you. I can confirm Orton Villas has come first in the Community Class, but you must wait until late September for all other results. Please remember that what I have told you is strictly confidential." Sam promised not to mention it to anyone except Lily.

Back to the local management, Bradley and Olga were taking more control on a day-to-day basis in lots of subtle ways. Remember, Olga was not Orton Villas' manager. She was a part-time manager at another local Sunshine Homes development, but at times, she discreetly used her influence over both Orton Villas and Bradley.

In fairness to Bradley, he did try to be helpful at times in the garden; for example, he allowed residents to uproot nine awful fir trees. These had been planted by the landscapers when the development was being built. They were then allowed to replace them with trees of their own choice. The trees were deciduous and were mainly spring blossom types. Even Bradley and Olga contributed.

As reported earlier, Bradley and his total demeanour were changing. He and Sam, in fact, had decided to hold a private meeting including Lily over their different views of how Orton Villas was being run. Sam felt that Bradley was patronising, very spiteful and certainly lacking in maintaining confidentiality with some residents. Gossip was rife and Bradley encouraged this, which caused a bad atmosphere. Sam and Lily believed that Bradley was suffering from OCD and was becoming a self-opinionated control freak.

"Oh!" Sam said, "He could go on."

So, a meeting with both Bradley and Helga was arranged. The meeting was arranged on neutral grounds. Sam and Lily talked about their concerns about the many rules and restrictions imposed on them by management. This had not been mentioned when they were buying the flat. Sam and Lily came away with a shake of hands. Management said they were only doing their job as they saw it and said Sam and Lily must attempt to understand this, but that they would be helpful in the future. Sam and Lily looked at eachother and Sam said, 'We shall see'.

Unfortunately, things did not run Sam and Lily's way at all and management continued as though they had never had a meeting. Seven residents were now alerted to the goings-on. They saw at many events, particularly at the evening social functions, how Bradley and Olga's control was getting stronger and also noticed that their intake of alcohol influenced their attitudes.

Clive, the handyman-gardener, was earning what appeared to be—from checking previous years' invoices—large sums of money, and not just on the garden. Other monies being spent were enormous, especially around the building.

In one instance, £700 were spent on the unused lane alongside the block of flats. Management discussed with Sam and Bert—he being a very useful and versatile neighbour—the possibility that between the three of them, they could obtain some large stone boulders—about 30—and cement them along the roadside grass verge. At the time, when Sam and Bert's labour was offered for free, the boulders would have cost £100 and cement £35. Bradley agreed on the proviso and what time they could spend on the project, said what a good and helpful plan it was, and asked them to go ahead.

Four days later, Bradley called Sam and Bert in his office. Clive the handyman-gardener had come up with another plan. He had acquired 75 shrubs costing with labour about £500. Bradley suggested that they take that offer. Sam and Bert realised they were beaten, so they reluctantly withdrew. What should have cost £135, cost a jolly lot more, including labour, etc. This was one of the many shared suspect projects carried out by Bradley and Clive, where they probably shared the spoils. Sam saw many invoices in the accounts of one year that raised these suspicions. Again, residents were never involved in any of these decisions, which was an example of 'I am in charge', and increasing domination over the residents.

It did not take long for many shrubs to fail because of poor ground preparations, just like the earlier experience of the lawn in the front garden turf. Naturally, these shrubs were to wither only to be replaced by the next new gardener in the manner originally planned. Boulders were now to be placed on grass. This was to stop vehicles from driving over the grass. This was to be another one of Bradley's follies—the £500 one. There were more!

Chapter 7

So continuing the story, Orton Villas still awaited the final Bloom results at Sunshine Homes. In the meantime, during late August, a letter arrived inviting up to four guests to attend the annual Royal Horticultural Society Southwest Bloom Awards in Cornwall. This was a very important annual event and a first for Sunshine Homes. This was to be a one-day presentation, which needed an overnight stay and also would allow Sam and Lilly and a new garden supporter, Sybil, to attend. They travelled by train.

A very well-known local BBC Gardeners' World presenter would present the awards. The main format was to present gold certificates and many other awards to towns and villages in the southwest region. Sam's town won a gold award for the second year running, and then came the surprise of the day; Sunshine Homes won an award for the Developing group. There were five awards in the group. They were awarded third out of five in this—the Community Class, the others being Outstanding, Thriving, Improving and Establishing.

It was a very proud moment for all three of them representing Sunshine Homes. What a success! Sam hugged Lily and Sybil excitedly. This was a real success, now they would tell many residents in the weekly newspaper of Sunshine Homes' gardening achievement. It took Sam back to only a few months back, when Bradley told Lily and Sam, "You really are too old to work in the garden," and, "I am responsible for all you do."

Both Sam and Lily looked at each other as they turned away with a 'tut tut'. They commented, "Hope he carries out a risk assessment then!"

What an achievement! Here was another certificate to take back to Sunshine Homes! The three of them stayed another night and celebrated with a nice evening meal and a glass of bubbly.

So, only a few evenings later, the time had arrived for the local bloom presentations in the local Rugger Club. As before, a bar was opened and lovely snacks were available. Olga requested Bradley not to attend as she needed help at Orton Villas with an evening function, a Quiz Night, and he would not miss anything of importance as he went last year. So, he asked Sam and Lily and three other residents to go instead. They said they would love to go, so they set off to the Rugger Club. Unofficially, Sam and Lily already knew that they had the Community first prize.

The evening proceeded and all sorts of cups and certificates were awarded. Finally, only one remained. It was larger than usual, and it was for the best garden display in the town. Everyone held their breath. The chairperson announced the results and the winner was Orton Villas. The five residents were jumping with joy and excitement.

"We've won, we've won!" they all cried. What a proud moment it was—their fourth award in two years.

Reminding readers that first, it was runner-up in the Community Class, followed by two awards a year later with the winners in the Community Class, then best in the town overall, followed by a developing award in the Southwest Awards. Here the winners enjoyed their success with yet again more photographs to come from the local newspaper.

After partaking of a lovely spread, all five residents came back to an empty Orton Villas. Everyone at the function had returned to their flats as it was 9 pm. Sam and Lily took both cups and certificates to their flat in readiness to show them to all the residents and Bradley at morning coffee.

On seeing the two certificates and, of course, the two gleaming silver cups, residents were really pleased. Bradley did not seem to share the same pleasure. However, various places were selected to hang the to-be-framed certificates, with pride of place—on the lounge fireplace—for the two cups.

A couple of days later, following a phone call to the local newspaper, a reporter called at Orton Villas to take more photographs of the awards. Naturally, many residents turned up for this occasion; as many as 16 or more went out into the garden. A few days later, there were the photographs to see in the local paper. The residents are reminded of it every time upon entering the Sunshine Homes building since there was a memorable photograph on the entrance wall.

On the surface, things did appear to be running smoothly at Orton Villas but beneath the surface, things were not. Bradley and Olga were still commanding more control. Clive, the handyman-gardener, was earning lots of money in both jobs he was doing: maintaining the building and also the garden. It was looking neglected, but then the management team there did not seem to have any real plan despite Bradley's occasional input. What a surprise! But then his team knew little about gardening, and they showed no real pride.

Perhaps, Sam was at an advantage with his garden knowledge. However, Bradley would bypass this because he was the manager. Once, when challenged and asked why there were no stripes on the lawn after cutting, he replied, "Clive cannot afford such luxuries I guess."

In a £5,000,000 development, what sort of answer was that?

Although Orton Villas' large garden, with its many colourful displays, always created an impact, the garden continued to lack proper seasonal maintenance. Lawn edges were never cared for, hedges always seemed to be cut in the wrong season, which had a bad effect on bird nesting time. Shrubs were also being cut in the wrong seasons.

One main concern, until pointed out to Bradley, was the apple blossom flower on the January flowering clematis—they were both side by side. Fred, Orton Villas' faithful and keen helper in the garden, was quick to point this out. It required lots of TLC. Also, in particular, two standard roses were bought. Assistance in planting was given as with many other shrubs in the garden to dead head and generally a little TLC and help in general, like weeding and lawn care. There were five to six residents who happily enjoyed such activity. No rota, just enthusiasm.

As this story continued to unfold repeatedly, the unrest continued and involved about eight to ten residents, not least from Barbara. The car park dilemma was always present. A few residents would talk quietly in corners but as expected, not aloud. If it was not the car park, it was the social evenings. Olga dominated at these events. Bradley was much quieter until the wine flowed, then his true colours would show!

Sam was continually keeping notes of many incidents that continued to occur because of the concerns of certain residents. In autumn, the garden was planted as normal, in readiness for the following spring. Soon, it was time to the plan for the summer. Excited residents were perhaps hoping for a repeat success of the previous year.

Chapter 8

There was a couple, Sid and Olive, who from day one, were different from all other residents. They were not involved in any of the community activities except a fish and chip supper on one occasion but never again, owing to health and safety issues raised by them both concerning the food and the cups (had they been washed properly?).

They developed their small garden plot in the form of a rockery in the rear car park area of the building. Everyone agreed to this separate feature and as a springtime garden, it was very attractive, but both Sid and Olive made it very clear to the rest of the house that they wished it to be their design and maintained by them. As they were 'loners', this request was agreed to. To this day, it remains an attractive and pleasant feature in the spring.

Readers may be trying to understand how come they were known as the house 'loners'. True to say, many of the residents would moan about what they would call injustices. Sam would be first in line if there were local disagreements and there were many, as Sam's story unfolds, we shall see those. Remember, Bradley, the manager, was influenced by his wife.

So back to Olive, we rarely saw Sid. Olive was always in Bradley's office with her clipboard, with many observations and 'complaints' all appertaining to various serious problems that she thought appropriately valid to discuss with Bradley.

Sam would say not necessarily to complain every time, but she was just observing how Bradley or Sunshine Homes were conducting their day-to-day business. Fine, some residents might even say that she became almost the house spokesperson.

She never got on with or spoke to Sam. In fact, she told Sam and Lily that she never ever wanted to speak to them. She certainly did not have many friends, but that did not bother her. Sam tried to hold out the olive branch many times, but when he was around, Sid would glare at Sam, telling him to go away. Truth be told, they regarded Sam and Lily as the enemies, as once again, later in our story, clashes developed between Olive and Sam over how the garden should be maintained. In Olive's rockery, the house agreed on its format of containing perennials and her voluntary funding, but in the main, they wanted bedding plants—which they contributed towards—but Olive disagreed. She argued that bedding plants were a waste of money because at the end of each season, they needed to be disposed of.

Therefore, the majority of the house enjoyed the colourful displays that appeared in all the 20 odd borders each season.

So, as a reminder of events, a new gardener was needed, and the evening social problems needed to be sorted out as Bradley and Olga insisted that they should run the social events.

So, first, there was the problem of a new gardener. The area manager Helga allowed house members to hold a meeting there. There was a massive support for someone with professional gardening experience. Later, as it was now July, final arrangements etc. would be made. Sam met the new gardener to make sure that this time, he was 'fit for purpose', and yes, he appeared to be. Sam reported back the good news and his appointment was confirmed. The commencement of his work was to be finalised in October. Bradley was not happy; Clive wasn't happy either, but it was the house's choice and Sam's recommendation. The house was paying for this arrangement, not them.

The issue of Olga and Bradley running the social events ended abruptly when Helga confronted Olga, told her that she had no right to be in control whatsoever or have anything to do with the social activity of the residents and requested that she resign.

Next day, at coffee, when Bradley announced the decision regarding the gardener, most of the residents were pleased about the new arrival, as both Bradley and Clive were not even gardeners to start with. More important was the fact that Bradley had said that Olga was gutted by her removal from the social committee. As it all transpired, all three: Bradley, Olga, and Area Manager Helga were made to agree to decisions made by the residents. This was a step in the right direction; the reins had been released a little.

Two major decisions were achieved and for the first time, in their favour. Interestingly enough, only a week earlier, Olga had had a confrontation with Joe, the chairman of the house committee, which resulted in Joe walking away in disgust, telling the other four members present that he was resigning because of Olga's manner. Olga, as usual, was a little 'bossy' and he was not prepared to listen to her. Sam was to report later that he also felt uncomfortable in Olga's presence and he would not be attending any more social committee meetings.

So perhaps this was Helga's reasoning for asking Olga to remove herself from the committee. The house residents could only reflect on Helga's decision but were not complaining. So, not unexpectedly, the remainder of the committee decided to disband as well. As a result, all social activity was regrettably abandoned. So, until further notice all social events were discontinued. A shame really! But upon reflection, Sam remarked that the socials should be run by the residents, not every month but on special occasions, some of which were coming up shortly.

From here on, Olga became a recluse because of this social decision. She then kept a low profile and was rarely seen by the residents. Sam thought that she was embarrassed; however, it was not an issue.

Soon it was September and the usual invitation came to attend the annual Bloom presentation. Five of the residents accepted and the date was booked.

Chapter 9

Previously, Sam had mainly talked about the concerns of the day-to-day running of the management structure and the concerns of the care of the large garden.

In the early days, on Bradley's watch, there were on average bi-monthly 16-seater coach trips. The driver would take them to local garden centres, National Trust properties and at Christmas time, a nice hotel for a Christmas lunch. One Christmas, the snow was so deep that the trip was cancelled and so four residents walked with great difficulty there and back, wearing Wellington boots plus their best clothes.

A large snowman was built in the front garden, which was captured in a photo and was later used to produce over 720 Christmas cards. Snow was quite rare in this part of Britain so you can imagine the hilarity of building a five-foot high snowman with a carrot for his nose, two pieces of coal for the eyes, a floppy black hat and a strip of leather for a smiley face. In fact, two young lads jumped over the wall, ran across the garden and knocked the snow man's head off. At first, Sam was cross, then Lily reminded him that they were all young once. It was soon repaired.

Then there was Anna, an American resident. She put up a notice—approved first by Bradley, naturally—to hold weekly yoga sessions for one hour. Initially, seven to eight residents responded; only five would turn up regularly. Sam and Lily also joined in. Everyone enjoyed the sessions; one resident was 90 years old. It ran for two years; unfortunately, it ended when Anna and her husband did not see eye to eye with Bradley and moved on elsewhere in the town. Once again, this was a major disappointment for the few residents there. It was just Bradley's attitude and his clashes with Anna that made them move on. If truth be known, he did not want them there doing yoga.

This was the first sign of a resident's clash with management. Sam, once more, was reminded by one or two residents of this unrest. In this instance, Bradley just wanted to be in control, and Anna wanted none of it. They were all mature people and Bradley's attitude in many instances was just not acceptable. Yes, Anna would not suffer fools gladly, but Bradley needed power!

Once again, as in previous autumn plantings, all went as before. Clive was beginning to show more support for Bradley, and as his manager naturally this would be correct; however, residents' requests were beginning to fall on stony ground again.

It was now early spring and three years on, all the usual plans were set in place for planting out in the garden.

It was also time to discuss with Bradley and Olga about when they should prepare and plant up the garden. Also, help from Clive would be appreciated, so this is what Sam discussed. Bradley listened along with Olga to Sam's suggestion in his office and all seemed harmonious. There were flowerbeds to empty and lots of rubbish to take away. Bradley said Clive would help where he could as he was busy. This was not what Sam wanted to hear. He and Lily were willing to help, but Clive was an important part of this physical task. Sam was feeling anxious as there was a lot to do, but he remained optimistic.

The very next day, Sam and Lily were doing yoga in Orton Villas' lounge when Bradley zoomed in, bent down and without any warning to the class, said aloud, "Clive will be on holiday for two weeks so he will not be able to assist you in the garden." Sam was annoyed to be told this way and stunned too. Was this the truth? Had Olga interfered? To all at Orton Villas, this was an important project. They were talking about a garden where timing was vital.

After this awful news from Clive, Bradley and Olga did help in the garden in the rain and began removing wallflowers and bulbs. Even Olive and Sid were doing similar tasks, but the two groups did not talk to each other. Sam's memory was vague as to why they were so helpful, but it was appreciated. Further planting was carried out as previously by their band of loyal helpers.

Looking back to that weekend in June of that third season, a large amount of friction was beginning to erupt. Sam was getting vibes from both the manager and his wife of a certain 'We do not want residents to be involved here' attitude. Then suddenly, another argument started between Bradley and Sam. The gist of it was: I know the exact spot. Bradley, very much in a bad mood and temper, said, "I will see that you never enter the local garden competition again." He was really annoyed.

So, behind the scenes, some house members felt that following Bradley's outburst, changes were afoot and that it was just a matter of time.

Eventually, the garden did get completed. It looked as good as ever. Then came a massive announcement from Bradley at coffee, which Sam and Lily no longer attended, "Our area manager Helga has told me that with immediate effect, all residents are banned from any activity in the garden whatsoever. No weeding, no deadheading, no planting, nothing."

This was music to Bradley's ears, even Olga's. Now, they had what they had waited for—control of every activity at Orton Villas and the social scene since there was no social committee. They also got control of the garden. These were the two main activities which would affect many residents—two members, Olive and Sid in particular. Remember, they were given written approval by senior management so that they could maintain their rockery, situated at the back of Sunshine Homes, alongside the car park.

They could not believe what Bradley was saying. Sid and Olive said that the rockery was a separate issue. Bradley continued to reiterate that it was not his decision, and senior management did not want a show garden and hoped in time all the bedding plant garden and the rockery garden would be controlled by Bradley and the newly appointed gardener.

The residents were very upset at the alleged decision of higher management. In general, there was much whispering in corners. Bradley now had what he needed—total control at Sunshine Homes in all areas.

So, although the large garden knew its future fate, there was still the general garden maintenance to take care of. The grass was in need of a lot of work because Clive, upset by his eventual removal, was 'on holiday'. The garden, where many photographs had been taken showing its current state, could be described as a meadow.

Chapter 10

A local garden provider came after many requests by residents, and photographs were captured to show how difficult and spiteful Bradley was becoming to Sam. This, in turn, began to affect Lily, and Sam needed medical assistance as this anguish was getting to him. Photographs were produced to show the meadow effect caused by erratic grass cutting. Before Clive went on holiday, Sam had brought to Bradley's attention the fact that hedge trimming should not be done in midsummer because of nesting birds. Too late! Clive had trimmed deciduous shrubs and bushes, which were now mainly bare. Garden knowledge was not one of Sunshine Homes' management's best attributes.

Sam, after discussing it with Lily, could not see a future in which residents could continue to be involved in the garden. Now, three other residents would also be made to cease activity. The day was a Wednesday, and Sam had called a meeting of all residents over the new developments concerning the garden. Sam had decided to resign from the social committee, as Joe had also resigned. This had a knock-on effect because the social committee also reluctantly disbanded. Now, there was no Joe, no Sam, and of course, no Olga. This meant all social events would cease.

So, with Bradley's permission, of course, Sam went ahead with the meeting. The lounge was packed with supporting residents. No surprise here then, over 40 residents were being banned from an award-winning garden.

Bradley, although not invited, was seen hiding behind a large pillar, close to his office. As usual, with Sam's presentation about to begin, everyone wanted to hear what he had to say.

Because of the total ban on any work in the garden, both Sam and Lily's work of planning, growing stock, etc. was now finished. There was an outcry as to why this was so, and more than one resident asked about it. Sam's reply was quick and simple. Sam thought that Helga, the area manager, and Bradley and Olga felt that the residents were controlling the garden activity. They were not interested in their success. They always had to be in control of everything, even fresh air, if it was possible. Control, possession, nothing was ever up for debate.

Of course, all three: Bradley, Olga and Helga had been trained in the art of persuasion, particularly Bradley. Sam suggested that he never actually told lies, but may have more than once withheld the truth. He certainly was very cunning, at times devious and certainly, the smiling enemy. It was also recorded, written by Helga, that whilst the garden was a lovely one in all its splendour, Orton Villas did not fit in with being a show garden. Health and safety meant that they were aged residents and were not capable of common sense, therefore this was the reason for the ban. An amazing supposition, as most magazines and health articles advocated how important gardening was for older people.

"Oh dear," said Sam, "is this retirement or mental cruelty?"

To allay fears of what was coming next, Sam immediately went on to talk about Clive, the alleged gardener. He was a handyman who cut grass. Bradley was not very knowledgeable about any gardening aspects either. He was interested in only saving money.

Taking a deep breath, Sam told his audience that as they will be getting the services of a new gardener in autumn, he had spent time working out a time spent schedule. He had done this at a positive cost per hour so many hours a week, therefore coming up with an annual budget. Finally, he asked that five regular residents with a large interest in gardening should be allowed to continue working in the garden. This would save £1,000 per year.

"Naturally," continued Sam, "for this plan to work, we would need both Bradley and Helga to approve. Whatever their decision, both Lily and I still may not be allowed our limited activity in the garden anyway." It was not to be. Later on, when Bradley was approached, once more he was emphatic and announced to Sam: "No one is to do any work in the garden at all. All residents are now banned."

Naturally perhaps, the house was split by this decision, but it was obvious to them that both managements had decided to take back the only decision not in their control. It was obvious that what Orton Villas may want, Sunshine Homes certainly did not. Bradley and Olga certainly would have felt happy now to be back in control at Orton Villas. As he sat down, Sam nervously commented, "Now I know how Diana felt with Charles and Camilla, just like I feel with Bradley and Olga."

Immediately, Bradley emerged from his listening hiding place behind the pillar, pointing fingers and shouting angrily, "How dare you tell such lies?" Boy, he was upset! Sam left the lounge immediately, but Lily stayed. An embarrassed Bradley, Sam was informed, went back to his office, on the phone at once with Olga, as was his daily routine. Was he angry? The truth always hurts.

A small note of interest: Olga failed to obtain the management position she had sought locally but secured a prominent position as a trainer of potential managers. It was still not her dream plan of seeing Bradley out; however, but a step in the right direction for her, as everyone at Orton Villas was aware.

Sam, along with a few loyal residents, was seeking a face-to-face talk with Helga. This was for him to ask again about the garden ban; particularly, how it would work with a new gardener and about Olga's influence on social events as now that there was no committee. The meeting date was arranged for a Friday in July. Just Sam, Lily and the area manager. No Bradley!

The answers they received from the area manager were not very promising.

The gardening ban was at Bradley's request (secretly Helga's as well) and as manager, his decision was, as expected, final. The social functions that were a concern to Sam had to come to an end.

This was a difficult situation. Some residents were not aware of any problems; some on the other hand, were. All future function dates were decided by Olga and Bradley in private. Also, decisions were taken as to which events would be held. Sam had evidence of this. One such occasion in particular concerned a local comedic act, which was refused without any discussion with the residents. There were others too.

Finally, a new gardener was to be appointed. The residents as well as Sam said that the current gardener was 'not fit for purpose'. Having given all the details to Helga, Sam was pleased when she said that investigations would be made over these allegations. They were checked, but the residents heard nothing, so the matter, as expected, was closed. Hence, the appointment of the new gardener was suspended.

Chapter 11

Earlier, Sam reported that if a garden ban was announced, Olive and Sid would be disappointed. Why? From day one, this couple was different from all other residents. They were not involved with the rest of the residents. They thrived on self-praise.

They developed, with written approvals—as previously mentioned—their own piece of garden. They also cared for it and it always showed. They would eventually blame Sam for the total garden ban, the grapevine hinted that might be the case.

Sam never found out why Olive was always in Bradley's office with her clipboard; Sam would say that she was not necessarily complaining every time, but observing how Bradley or Sunshine Homes were conducting their day-to-day business. Fine, some residents might say that she became almost the house spokesperson, but she never got on with or spoke to Sam. She certainly did not have many friends but that did not bother her. Sam tried many times to hold out an olive branch to her, but to no avail.

However, there came an opportunity for the house to save a lot of money, thanks to Olive. She worked hard to have a financial problem resolved; it was with regard to the warden's rent that they paid. The flat builders requested a very high annual rent, not compatible with the area, in fact. Olive, after a strong battle with the powers, secured a reduction of £4,000 per annum; however, Orton Villas did lose the occupant rent that was originally the cost of visitors using the residents' guest room.

In future, all guest monies would be given to the landlord, which at the time, lost them approximately £2,000 per annum. The (warden) manager still had to maintain the guest room as part of his brief. At least, they received a small rebate as a token of goodwill, £50. This charge still represented over £1,000 per month rental charge paid by the residents for the warden's flat. An exorbitant charge! Olive was bestowed with a lot of praise as well as appreciative words for her effort.

As time passed, Olive always had something to see the warden about, and she always had the clipboard in her hand, but she meant well.

Chapter 12

So in the meantime, early in August, Sam set out with a miserable-looking Bradley. Sam had arranged to meet the new professional gardener again, which he did. Bradley shook hands with Dave, the new gardener and immediately said, "Can't stop. Can I leave this with you?" He was not helpful and seemed a little sulky. Why would he not be? Clive was on his way out of his gardening job, but of course he would still be working closely with Bradley as his caretaker-type assistant.

So, Dave took Sam around some gardens and Sam saw all the modern equipment, two mowers, one with a roller, and was impressed. After a cordial discussion of starting dates, his pay was agreed upon, but Dave was told earlier, in no uncertain terms, by Bradley that all residents were completely banned from working in the garden. As expected, some residents were not very happy, even when the then supportive regional manager was somewhat sympathetic. Bradley and Helga—in their collusion—had the power to keep all residents out, especially Sam. The grapevine said that a few residents had also requested this. This will, as the story develops, show that power, possession and jealously prevailed at Orton Villas.

So, one Thursday evening in late September, it was the Rugger Club Bloom awards evening. Following the preparations in June, they would very possibly lose. Both Bradley and when he turned up, Clive were not very helpful in the garden's preparation. This did not help the residents who were waiting to plant the garden. This was when Bradley said to Sam, "I will see that Orton Villas never enters this competition."

The normal procedure of the award being presented was repeated. Like the years before, suddenly the presenter called out: "And the Community Award goes to Orton Villas." The five residents in the party went wild with excitement. Five awards in three years! Second in Community, Community winners in the following year, two awards in Community, outright town winners a year later, and finally, the RHS award in Newquay.

Eat your heart out Bradley and Area Manager Helga, they all thought. Once again, all five of them came to an empty lounge, but they were full of happiness. Five awards in three years. Unprecedented! Ringing in Sam's ears was Area Manager Helga's voice saying, "We do not want a show garden here, no thanks."

Sam said to Olga, "You and Bradley are frightened that you may be losing something you desperately need: power!"

Early next morning, on the lounge mantelpiece alongside another Community Award certificate, stood the lovely cup and there was more! At coffee, a real bombshell fell. As normal, the usual chat took place, then Bradley announced, "I see the cup, surely we don't need to wallpaper my walls any more with cups and certificates. You have won them all, we do not want any more!" His words echoed in Sam's ears. Remember, Bradley had said earlier, "I will see that you do not enter the Bloom completion ever again."

The residents were stunned but were accustomed to not saying anything as Bradley was the boss. What he or Olga said, was law. Now, of course, there would be no more awards. Remember, all residents were now banned from the garden. But readers, this was not the end, it was not even the beginning of the end, but perhaps the end of the beginning. (Churchill)

One of Sam's relatives was so upset by Bradley's ban that he arranged to meet a local newspaper and told the whole story to them.

Well, guess what? Yes, a week later, on the front page were capital letters saying, 'Blooming Spoilsports' in the headlines and the full story of the ban.

The reactions of the residents were incredible. Some very strong words of indignation came from Bradley at coffee. "It is all lies," he yelled, "You know, we all know where this has come from." He meant Sam. "I will consult with my solicitor." Bradley continued, "For any residents agreeing with me, I have some hand-made circulars, a type of complaints form. I will not stand for this accusation, I will show him!"

Of course, Sam was not present but was aware of what was going on. His relative had forewarned Sam of what to expect. Whatever Bradley was preparing to do was of no consequence. What was written was the truth for all readers in the town to see. This was yet another little publicity, which following on from the newspaper featuring their garden awards, was not to do them any harm. Finally, we will see again as the future story will eventually show that there was a much bigger bombshell coming.

Also, Olga was now established as a qualified trainer under Helga's control. Bradley was becoming more influenced by them and Olga was still looking towards replacing Bradley as manager. Sam was not making these stories up, remember, he was writing down all sorts of comments and listening to others very regularly. Sam told close friends, even those who did not live at Orton Villas, firstly how controlling Bradley was and about Olga's removal from the social committee, and although there were no functions being held, there was still the daily running of the site. The car park problem surfaced nearly every day; at times, this was very stressful. Residents would deliberately not go out in their cars for fear of losing their spot. Barbara was also complaining about her 'spot'. Bradley took no notice. Physically, yes, they argued a lot but inwardly, it might have needed some understanding.

However, this story should be about residents and their needs, not about management and their problems. Do readers need reminding that both managers were well paid and were living in a luxury two-bedroomed flat in a fantastic location and parking their car every day in the privileged manager's spot?

'Mr Mannering', as Bradley became known, was really becoming obsessed with power.

Security of course! Bradley actually said that to prevent a large, hairy man nipping in and stealing the residents' purses, they were no longer allowed to exit via the patio doors that led into the lovely garden. Fear again! They were told that the doors would only be allowed to be opened if Bradley was available on site. Considering his working schedule was for 35 hours a week out of 168, there would be limited opportunities for residents to exit the doors.

Then, to enter the lovely garden, a long detour was necessary. Once more, this was Bradley's obsession for power. Often Sam would ask Bradley why he could not provide all residents with the same main door entry key as used 24/7 to ensure the door would be self-locked. Bradley refused to listen to the argument. Once more, he was dictating. It was all about control!

When it rained, water entered under the glass doors, the carpet became soaking wet and he refused to have a soak away fitted (this could have been billed as a fault in the building works and rectified for free). But no, Bradley was in his stubborn mode. Money again! He always refused to have a small soak away put in because of the cost. He was extremely frugal on matters of cost unless he had caused the problem (Twice with the water pump, Clive's garden budget). Sam and others suspected that an annual bonus incentive regarding the budget came into play here.

So, Bradley continued to be as spiteful as ever. Only one month earlier, suddenly early one morning, there appeared a note on the manager's door which said that for health reasons, Bradley and Olga were taking two weeks' respite. The manager was to be on duty care. Well, well! Was this that they both were at last feeling the pressure? At the time, many residents wanted to know more. Although residents were asking, Sam and a few others were whispering, "Is he beginning to weaken because of us?"

One resident said, "He will not be too over-troubled; a leopard will never change his spots."

Whatever. Something was going on. Also, as per usual, because of cost, there was no relief manager. Why? Because the powers that be were very good at persuading residents that one was not required. Sam at the time said this was not a cynical remark. It was true. He had witnessed it at earlier meetings. To be honest, because of Bradley's salesman approach, there was not a true local voice there. Later, Sam said that in time, he would talk more about a relief manager.

Sheep's health and safety come to mind, Sunshine Homes' philosophy was to keep the residents in a pen, treat them like sheep and keep them under control. Sam said this was what residents felt and many said it but were too aged to shout out these sort of feelings.

Chapter 13

By November, the struggle continued and a sort of arrangement was organised regarding social events.

It was not a committee as such. Bradley and Olga joined up with one other resident and one or two would assist not in preparing the lounge but with function ideas, a sort of unofficial committee, mainly to discuss things in their flat. Sam had heard of these arrangements and said he did not know how many or when these meetings took place, but they did. The time, place and date were always decided by Bradley and Olga. Was Helga turning a blind eye to this move?

As could be seen by many, after the garden and social events, the management was now in control of the glass doors and their opening as well. Coming off, the social committee did not stop Olga's involvement. These events were bingo, raffles, bring and share, and speakers. Oh yes, Olga was very adamant and certainly in control despite her removal from the abandoned committee.

These events in the early days encouraged up to 26 residents, but gradually this fell to about 12 to 15. There was only one male in the end, not that this made much difference. Sam and Lily also left for obvious reasons.

So Sam's unrest continued and then came the saddest day since his arrival. It was early November, when he and Lily met up with Helga and explained to her their concerns about Bradley and Olga's control and how, in their view, Orton Villas was not overall a happy place anymore. The house was split, and certainly its spirit had died—all because of such obsessive control. So, they told Helga that they would resign from everything to do with Orton Villas. They would put their intentions on the house notice board. Specific letters were to be delivered to special friends. Incidentally, later they received a few letters of thanks for their endeavours at Orton Villas soon to become their—I repeat—their garden of destruction.

A few days later, a good friend and neighbour, a spokeswoman, spoke to Sam about all this anguish, "We guess you must be bitter and upset."

"Yes," Sam replied, "very."

Helga had given Sam the impressions of 'good, it is all over now. Perhaps Bradley can get on to do work for which he is paid.' In other words, good riddance. In Sam's head, there were two signals regularly coming and going: it is not over till the fat lady sings, and management may think it's all over, "But wait," said Sam, "we will see."

Note readers, remember what Sam said.

After all this activity, Sam and Lily went off overseas to their first grandson's christening. They were away for a few weeks and on their return, they had received two letters, one from Helga wishing them well, tongue in cheek.

The second was from a solicitor, Barbara's in fact. It said that Sam was invited at Barbara's request to help support her with a statement on her behalf in a claim of harassment by Manager Bradley. Also, he was requested to attend a court summons in mid-March. Enclosed was a formal request to attend court on the specific date. Also, there was a cheque for £50 towards expenses.

Sam could not believe what he had just read! He called Lily, and they both decided to send a statement in support but refuse court attendance and return the expense cheque for £50, and that would be the end of the matter. This is what they did. Two days later, another letter with no cheque inside arrived containing a court summons demanding his attendance. Incidentally, I forgot to mention whilst they were away, there was a court date postponement because of their trip overseas a few weeks earlier.

Apparently, this was due to all the conflict over parking over the months. Bradley was fed up with Barbara's continual complaining about the car park. He claimed that she continued to harass him. There was a simple explanation. If only he, in her words, was prepared to be firstly helpful and show her more empathy, this could have been resolved. He, on the other hand, was always adamant that he could not help her. First come first served was the car park rule.

Therefore, her harassment was unnecessary so he had no alternative but to take her to court. The reason: harassment. As previously mentioned, Barbara was totally disabled. It was better for her to continue to park outside her flat with total comfort than park elsewhere if there was a space. Often, there was not. Hence the continued bickering. In Sam's opinion, he was being a bully and jobsworth!

So Barbara, Sam and Lily were summoned to attend court before a judge. Bradley, as they knew he would, obtained 14 witnesses and their statements from the residents who also attended the court. Barbara, Bradley and Helga were the only persons to be called before the judge. Lily and Sam were invited into an anteroom, the 14 witnesses just sat outside the courtroom and waited. One and a half hours later, all three of them emerged. Barbara was smiling but not Bradley. Olga was embracing him in a sympathetic cuddle.

Before the judge's report was delivered, perhaps a short reminder is needed as to why they were summoned to attend court in the first place. Sam had said many times in Barbara's defence how disabled she was, and not to put too fine a point on the subject, she would need a little empathy as to her vulnerability, not concerning her driving. However, when she arrived, there were not many residents parking cars. So obviously, she chose the spot near her front door, or even at the end of a row so that she could get out conveniently on her right-hand side.

Unfortunately, Bradley did not suffer fools gladly (he really was a bully), and he often referred to Barbara as the woman who was always complaining.

"No, I am not!" she would retort. When she would return in the evenings, often there were no free spaces in the back, only five in the front of the building. If there were, she couldn't walk far. Bradley knew that. Then if the park was full, it was impossible for her to walk from there. So yes, she did complain often when confronted by him. It would have been nice if he was more helpful but he was not. He just thought she was a complainer. Sadly, senior management agreed with him.

So, this harassment charge from Bradley was not really necessary. Apparently, the judge's report was as follows: both parties must—unless in an emergency—refrain from any form of direct conversation for six months. A court order would follow if this was not complied with. The judge also said that Bradley's request for the case to go to a higher court would be at a prohibitive cost so common sense would need to prevail.

So as a result, it cost Barbara a lot of money to defend herself and it was a shame that it went like that. Bradley, well, it probably cost him nothing except loss of pride, but still he, no doubt, would soon overcome even that. Barbara left happy. As Sam and Lily were driven home, they chatted over the events. The silence would be good, a little forced peace from both parties. Naturally, the 14 persons who voluntarily attended the court were very disappointed with the outcome from the judge, but as it is often said, 'Truth will always come out in the end.' 'Compromise' must have been in the judge's mind.

Next day was a Friday coffee morning as usual. There stood Bradley, no normal cocky smile, though. He started off by saying how disappointed he was with the judge's decision. He had asked Helga for approval to go further with his case. This request was turned down because of higher expected costs. Monies that the judge considered would be money squandered, especially as it was not a high court case. The judge said that it would be a waste of money. Hence Bradley's disappointment. Rumour, gossip, whatever it was, alleged that it had cost £10,000 just for Bradley to go to court.

Sam later said without sounding vitriolic, "This result was good." For the first time in three years, someone had said no to Bradley, it must have hit him hard, losing this important issue of control. Barbara went away on holiday to recover from Orton Villas.

As all this news was unravelling, the regional manager then became involved. He telephoned Sam and asked for a meeting with him and Lily in the city at a convenient city centre hotel. This was early spring. Why the meeting? Well, for months now, Sam had tried to get his regional manager to respond to his concerns about how Bradley was running Orton Villas. This was a very important decision for them both. So, a meeting was quickly arranged and they met the regional manager.

Firstly, they were put at ease, and then coffee was ordered. Sam began talking to the regional manager from carefully prepared notes. Sam started talking about how Bradley was very efficient at all aspects of running the building. Sam never suggested that he may have OCD, as the house and building were always neat and tidy and well looked after. Bradley, with Olga's influence, was always in control.

Unfortunately, it was his total demeanour. He was only medium built, not extremely tall and always came over firstly like 'I am always right'. He had a strong personality and a way with words. Sam stated that he was also extremely persuasive, almost a bully. The house never made decisions to suit the silent majority but a few brown-envelope residents, the residents who would exchange favours with Bradley. They were the ones who supported Bradley over Sam and enjoyed the gossip. Following the garden ban, the few who agreed with Bradley showed contempt for Sam by refusing to speak to him. It was reciprocal. Looking back, it is clear that the whole situation was created by Bradley because of his continual jealousy and fear of losing control over the house.

So often the silent majority were too frightened to speak out. If they did, the area manager Helga, along with Bradley, would pay lip service to resolving many of their claims. In fairness to Olive (Clipboard Clara) she could be seen nearly every day in or around Bradley's office, suggesting one thing or another. She was a loner. She rarely consulted anyone else and at area manager's meetings, she would talk for England—boring at times, occasionally with common sense. Sam's regional manager was writing notes and was expressing concern over the comments that were being made.

Then Sam said that there were six other residents who would at least like, if only by telephone, to talk to him. The regional manager agreed to what was being said, all names and telephone numbers were passed over, and he gave a promise that he would contact these six people.

After a good two hours chat, they bid their farewells. Both Lily and Sam were so pleased that they felt for the first time that they now had someone who was listening. Both Sam and Lily considered it really a 'coup' for a very busy man to consider their problems so seriously when many thousands of other residents in the southwest region were under his control. Were they alone? Or was this a common problem? The area

manager was responsible for as many as 1, 200
residents in just her area and there were probably 30
such Sunshine Homes in the region. Luckily, however,
they had found someone who was obviously concerned
and wanted to help.

Chapter 14

Within a few days, five residents had each received a phone call. It took a little extra time to make contact with the sixth person. Details of all the calls were conveyed personally by telephone to Sam, who was very pleased. All the residents' concerns were aired to the regional manager, no confidences were broken, and Sam reported that they were totally happy that their concerns had been listened to and had been logged, should they be needed in the future. Who knows, they might be?

On reflection, his story—whilst all true—is at the moment, a little out of sequence.

Please bear with me if when reading this story, this is noticeable. A reminder of where we are at: Sam and Lily have had their face-to-face meeting with their regional manager, return phone calls have been made, Olga has been removed from the social committee, she is gutted, and there is no committee now. Bradley and Olga still control everything. So, now Sam will continue his story.

It was June, the annual anniversary of the development. In previous times, they always held a fish and chip supper but not this year. The house was told that the management would be away that weekend so they would hold it the following weekend. There was no choice, they were just told.

Then a resident said, "But that is the queen's jubilee weekend. We have all requested a cream tea."

"That can be held the following weekend," they replied, and that was that. Both these decisions showed how Sunshine Homes' management was in control. This was just how their lives were. Back to that way of persuasion.

"Help us! We are losing control despite the regional manager's intervention," Sam asked the listeners among the residents, "Where is our independence going?"

In conversation with residents from Bradley's previous flat just up the road, they realised that this was just how the pair of them operated. They were described as a wicked pair. Olga was not a house manager then, but she was just as bossy.

So, now some 30 letters and emails had been sent to management with a limited response. Where do we go next?

The Sunshine Homes Ombudsman was the next step, where it was claimed they would have a fair hearing. They should be so lucky!

For a start, they never had a face-to-face meeting.

Their complaint was heard by Human Resources' select representatives who must have just read a report and dismissed it. On reading their reply, Sam and Lily were extremely disappointed as this was not a fair way to do business in their opinion. It simply read: no further action was necessary and that the complaints procedure was carried out as per Sunshine Homes' procedure. Also, on a personal note, the current CEO wrote a thank you for all the garden success. "I am about to retire and I wish you well for the future," the letter read.

"Oh no, you don't," the house said. So a relative took up the baton.

Sam and Lily were devastated. A personal phone chat was arranged by a relative with the outgoing CEO who was in on the Human Resources committee. They were never privileged to know its content, it was confidential. All they were told when the CEO moved on was, "There are changes coming, all will be told when I have gone." When the new woman CEO arrived later, another relative took up the baton. She emailed her complaint to the new CEO, a reply came, concern was mentioned, and a report was said to be sent soon with all the results and issues.

Sam was heard to say, "It is not over till the fat lady sings."

While waiting for a reply from their relative, Sam and Lily arranged to see their local MP in the locality. It was now July. When they arrived to see him, his secretary was also present. The MP listened, while the lady present typed away all their woes. The MP was shown the photo album of their successful garden achievements, told about the garden ban, the bullying and entrance and exit prevention to the garden via glass patio doors. Lots of other events had taken place that Sam and Lily explained about in detail.

After about 20 minutes, the MP asked his secretary, "Have you got all that down? Please now send it to the Sunshine Homes' CEO, adding my concerns about the welfare of my residents and other residents."

They thanked the MP for his time and concern, he replied, "I will keep you informed of the developments."

Sam and Lily left feeling again that someone of importance had listened to their plight. Remember readers, these two residents had gone down many routes: manager, area manager, regional manager, a retiring CEO, a new CEO, Age Concern, a solicitor, Citizens' Advice and now their local MP, still they were yet to see the police. As yet, whilst all these services visited were sympathetic and were very concerned about the alleged situation at Orton Villas, there was not a lot that could be done. Sunshine Homes ran their business as they saw fit.

So with all this negativity around Sam and Lily, there was still one option left for them. Move!

Now the house was aware of their intentions about walking away from Sunshine Homes, not just the various committees, but the garden, would they move elsewhere? They were secretly hoping for a rescue plan. Early in August, Sam and Lily were successful in obtaining a meeting with Area Manager Helga. Sam hoped for a compromise. Hopefully, Helga would agree to not planting but assisting the gardener with the various jobs at certain times.

The three were in Bradley's office, discussing their plan when Bradley just entered and interrupted the conversation three times. One of these was for some Sellotape. He was being possessive, jealous, downright rude and most importantly, noisy. Helga did not promise much, but declared, "I will have a word with Bradley. After all, he is your manager."

Typical Bradley! He was obviously listening at the door. Was he getting worried?

Eventually, they both left the office, slightly optimistic.

It was now early August, and following the meeting, Bradley was heard talking to Helga. The result was again, 'Under no circumstances must they work in the garden.' In other words—banned! This was another spiteful decision. Why? Because in the Sunshine Homes magazine, there were photographs, and articles written about how residents across the country clubbed together not only to buy but also plant up residents' gardens, and not always using the services of the regular gardeners. Whilst there at Orton Villas, the residents had done a similar programme and had received five awards in three years in regional and local competitions but because of the jealous whim of management, they were banned. Thanks Bradley, Olga and Ice Maiden Helga.

Upward and onward! Then a stroke of good fortune!

It was Thursday, mid-August.

Chapter 15

A colleague asked Sam to phone the local paper's office and ask for so and so and ask a local journalist to meet him. Sam thought about it and had a chat with Lily. They both decided to ask their brother-in-law to make the contact, this would enable them to keep a low profile. So this was arranged. Sam's brother-in-law was brought up to speed. Also, he had the garden's photograph album and was told of the forced ban from any activity in it. Also, a brief history of residents' overall unrest and of how they were treated was given.

Their brother-in-law reported back and said how pleasant his meeting had gone. The reporter was extremely interested in their story. He said it would certainly go to print in the next weekly paper and to watch out for it. The residents at Orton Villas could not wait; they were so full of excitement and anticipation. It was 8 am, the day they had been waiting for, and the paper arrived.

There on the front page in bold print were the headlines, 'Blooming Spoilsports'. Sam and Lily, after reading the full report, were beside themselves. They were later heard reporting, "It reminds us of the Noel Edmonds Show and how often he would say 'Gotcha'!" This is what both Sam and Lily wanted to say to Bradley and Olga. This was a little payback for all the misery they were causing.

Anyway, the reaction from Bradley was yet to come. Next day was a Friday, coffee morning. In came Bradley, all guns firing, "Have you seen the local weekly paper? It is full of lies, don't you agree? You all know it is!"

Bradley was almost frothing at the mouth, "Our solicitors are on the case. It is libel, and we all know who is responsible. We will get him," screamed Bradley. "In the office," shouted Bradley, "there are specially prepared complaint forms." Yes, they were on Bradley's own notepaper, not on Orton Villas—all panic and white lies. There were a few residents who requested these unofficial complaint forms. Oh yes, Bradley still continued to hold court with some supporters.

In the short term, some people said so what, but Sam and Lily had won a claimed victory as later readers will see. One massive side effect was that even three years on, seven flats were now selling as cheap as chips. If residents wanted to move, they were now trapped because of the incredible fall in the resale prices. Many of them had no buyers, maybe Orton Villas was jinxed.

Bradley's anger was not unexpected. Orton Villas' residents learnt a little more, but not publicly and all these stories were now adding up. Talking around outside, whether it be at the doctor's or in the local shops, the locals were talking of the rumoured unrest at Orton Villas. This was the sort of news senior management did not want to hear, and as Sam remarked to residents, this meant more people could now be listening.

However, deep in Sam and Lily's hearts was total dismay. Yes, management may now be listening but no real notice was taking place on their behalf. If it was, they were not aware of it.

With deep regret, having seen another property for sale minutes away, Sam and Lily called in the local estate agents, with a view to moving on from Orton Villas. They both had to accept a resale price of £60,000 less than the original cost, and all this after only four years! As events would turn out, prices would drop a lot more. Residents were not aware of any of this until the advert appeared in the local paper. It was a shock to some residents.

It was now early September. Both Sam and Lily were under no illusions regarding them selling quickly. Naturally, they were keen for the sale. They had both visited the new property twice but had received no response for their property as the agent had suggested that it was a really bad time. Locally, news was out about the goings-on at Orton Villas. Then of course, as previously stated, Orton Villas' reputation did not help. The agent was surprised to hear their comments regarding Bradley, as he came across as being of a good sort of manager, in fact, such a lovely man. As expected, there was disappointment since they did not even receive one reply from the paper advert. Therefore, Sam and Lily had to withdraw their offer on the property they had seen.

Where to now? they both thought. The police. This suggestion came from the estate agent, ex-police herself. When Sam and Lily told her of all that they had endured, she was thinking with her ex-police women's thoughts whether there was any legal action that the police could help with. So with the advice they were given, a phone call to the local police station was arranged, and sure enough, yet another female police officer made a call to them and a meeting was arranged.

So, late one September evening, the local police lady turned up. After nearly two hours of detailed reports and seeing pictures of their five times winning Town Bloom competitions, the police lady said, "I will now investigate what you have told me." She recorded it all and said, "I will get back to you." Within a couple of days, she did.

She talked to the area manager, who told the police lady that they were only carrying out normal procedures in line with management agreements as far as Orton Villas was concerned. Therefore, in the opinion of the company, they had done nothing wrong. Likewise, the police lady's hands were tied from pursuing the case further. Sam and Lily were given a log number, which was the normal police procedure apparently, and they began reflecting on what was their next step.

They had mentioned common law. When normally one buys into a service, like buying a new car or a bottle of tomato sauce, and if one has a complaint or is not satisfied over an issue, then one would hope that someone would do the right thing to help solve it. This was all Sam and Lily were seeking in many residents' opinion, but they were continually being fobbed off by company rules. Certainly, a lack of empathy was always present.

While writing this story, Sam felt that their situation was not unlike that of Nelson Mandela's situation in South Africa. The difference being that his was political and theirs at Orton Villas was controlling and mental bullying behaviour towards older people.

Chapter 16

Moving on disappointed, then a little concerned about the story of the lady who was particularly seen most early mornings hanging around supplying coffee, etc. outside Bradley's office. Sam never implied anything, but it did become the usual gossip that was anything going on, especially when the most common information written on the board was 'checking the building and on site'. Bradley came over as a chancer. To add to this chatting was what sort of impact did the newspaper article have on him, Olga and Helga?

If Bradley was in the office in presence of the lady with the door open whilst he was talking to her, he would shuffle papers. Even worse, he would listen behind the large concrete pillars, in fact anywhere if there was gossip. 'Nosey' should have been his nickname. The residents would often refer to him as 'Mr Mannering'. Remember the recent office chat with Helga when he kept popping in? The situation was now at a stage where some residents refused to talk to Sam and Lily, two even asked them not talk to them. The house would gossip continually more and more lately.

About nine residents were on Bradley's wavelength. How sad! Once, everyone was community-minded but not now. A few residents had died, four in fact had moved off, unable to cope with the day-to-day bickering.

Reminding everyone, September was still in focus. Bradley and Olga thought that they had most of the residents in the palm of their hands. They believed that no one could ever get them out of Orton Villas. *Wishful thinking*, thought Bradley.

Sadly, Sam remembered all the residents who had listened to his comments, all he had tried to do was tell the truth about all the problems. Even Barbara had called the police earlier, with no luck. She was also given a log number and everything was written and recorded because of how Bradley would continue to, in her words, bully her. At times, she would tell Sam that normal people just would not believe how she was treated.

Sam did concern himself, most residents were aware of the situation. A few said that she was a troublemaker and wished that she would move on. Towards the end of the month, Sam had a message that mentioned that Helga had suggested that Sam, Lily and Bradley listen to an independent mediator. This was agreed in early October, the meeting was with two professional people: a male and a female and to be held in their respective flats at the end of October. Wow! So someone had listened to Sam and Lily— mediation, a live meeting with two independent arbitrators and in their own flats. The same for Bradley. This was a major break-through.

At this time, Sam also got a reply from his MP. The email which was sent recently was just to say that everything was in hand. Also, Barbara had been able to talk on the telephone to Sunshine Homes' regional manager about all her woes. She was given permission to have a new lock fitted on the patio door to enable easier access. Earlier, this was turned down by Bradley as Sam had recorded previously and like many other requests, Bradley's 'Noes' became 'Yeses'.

Gosh! It seemed as if everything was happening all at once. The regional manager, at Sam's request, agreed once more to see them, this time in their flat, on a date in early October. Readers may recall they last conversed in March.

This really was a coup—two regional manager visits in six months. It may become historical as later the following year, he would also resign.

It may be of interest to some, but this day was the 442nd day since Sam had started his campaign for fairness with Helga, the very cold-mannered area manager.

Chapter 17

Sam was thinking whether the saga would ever end. Reflecting on the amount of time that had been spent over what Orton Villas' residents called a 'Carriage of Injustice', the interview day arrived. Sam and Lily invited their regional manager into their home.

Just like the meeting in March, Sam was prepared with a plan. Due to his old days in a previous life, presentations were his forte. Also, Sam was fully aware of how Bradley, Olga and Helga were a strong team and could present a strong case of persuasion that what Orton Villas' residents were saying was not true and that most things were running smoothly. Helga gave the impression that she supported residents on her very rare visits but they were also aware that Orton Villas' management and his wife were definitely in full control of everything.

So, Sam began his presentation. It was another episode about life at Orton Villas based on facts, truth, and records of receipts and invoices about various aspects of the day-to-day running of Sam's retirement home.

With a little emotion in his voice, he talked about himself. How he never passed his 11 Plus examinations, therefore had no grammar school academia, how before he was 15 years old, he did a morning and evening paper round, how he helped the local milk man deliver to households loose milk in jugs, not bottles, and how he was also trusted to collect cash.

This was not a university of learning academia. This was the beginning of the University of Life. It taught him to be reliable, honest and positive, and that hard work would bring rewards for effort. He learnt to criticise but constructively and to know the value for money, fairness and most importantly, empathy. There was not much of any of that at Orton Villas. "Oh!" said Sam, there was much more. Two years National Service RAF and a City and Guilds five-year apprenticeship.

Then, Sam moved on to accounts. These, he said, had caused him much concern. Clive earned large sums of money, all with Bradley's approval, in the past year, and not just in the garden but also all around Orton Villas as well. On scrutinising the annual accounts, Sam also saw many job dockets to do various works, some that were attempted more than once.

Like the futile attempt when there was water on most wet days—Bradley would lay towels regularly to soak up the water running under the glass patio doors. Anyone else could see that a metal grid under the doors would allow the water to simply be prevented from entering the building. Clive must have spent many pounds on several occasions, attempting to rectify the problem. Bradley just would not get a proper builder in to do the necessary work. These were his continual attempts to keep down costs. Soon after which, a new carpet had to be laid.

He really did think, thought Sam, *that he was spending his own money frugally and not the house's.*

This was like the aborted hedge work outside the side door and the laying of the old front car park turf. Now, three years later, it was obvious that it was a total disaster. Manager Helga told residents that despite its 'brown colour' the grass was fit for purpose as Bradley had said when he laid the turf originally.

Clive had worked February to September in the garden and was kept very busy through the rest of the year. Sam did show the regional manager the invoices of the amounts, but those cannot be printed here.

Also shown were the various telephone calls, in particular, to a European country regarding a private flat for sale there at Orton Villas, showing that these calls were made at least five times from Bradley's office. These were personal calls and should have shown that they were paid for separately. They never were. Therefore, these private and personal calls were paid for by the residents at Orton Villas. The house never witnessed as promised a list of all private calls. This was proof that Bradley was also avoiding payment of any private calls. Bradley was never challenged over these and perhaps many other calls made at other times.

So, Sam had given evidence to the regional manager of what was going on and clearly showed the high volume of spending. The meeting closed after one and a half hours. Both Sam and Lily were seemingly satisfied with the outcome. The regional manager also seemed satisfied with the meeting. Sadly, they never saw him again. Did Sam and Lily make an impact? We shall see.

The day arrived when they would meet the two mediators. A knock at the door told Sam and Lily that a lady and a gentleman had arrived. They knew they were visiting them first.

As they sat and settled, coffee was accepted. The couple were in their 60s and appeared as they expected mediation-type people to look like: soft spoken, and very calm. As they both listened to their tales of woe, they were very interested in the photograph album, which was where Sam and Lily began their story.

Firstly, why they moved to Orton Villas and the joys of the shared success in winning five Bloom competitions in three years because of Sam's horticultural background. Then, they told them about the disappointment when their management team declared, "We do not want a show garden here at Orton Villas," and then the consequences of the residents being banned from the garden completely.

Then, there was the bullying, deceit and total abuse of management control. Also, Bradley was married to a warden at another establishment and she held a heavy control there at Orton Villas. At this point, Sam broke down, there was almost a tear. They had come here to have a relaxed retirement, not all this disappointment and hassle.

After three quarters of an hour (the specific time allowed), the couple turned to each other and said, "With the many other problems you have outlined, we must finish now, but we can assure you that we have taken onboard all that you have told us. We will keep you informed of further developments." So the two mediators left and then went to hear Bradley's side of the story.

Sam had also mentioned the concerns over the relief manager and how residents were persuaded—allegedly without pressure—that the very low budget was sufficient for Orton Villas' needs. The truth was that the agreed amount helped keep the annual budget down and again, there was no proof, but the residents suspected that the annual budget was incentivised in some way for the management.

The amount of the relief manager's annual budget was always subject to conjecture. The official amount allowed was approximately £600 per annum. Sam could not ever remember any money of that amount ever being discussed and put aside. Yes, there was £360 which was always available—if it was needed—being put aside for this cover. This would then certainly keep the budget down overall.

Such was Bradley's control, that the area manager Helga would surrender her discussion of the official budget to him. Such was his power. This would represent just two weeks' cover for holidays etc.

Those at Orton Villas were regularly put on the helpline. This was the emergency call for assistance button. This was the out-of-hours system. Of note, it was after 5 pm daily till 9 am, five days and on weekends. The system actually ran from 5 pm Friday till 9 am Monday, hence management was only on site 48 hours a week out of 168 hours.

When Bradley was on site out of hours—more than once certainly—Sam was called out, not Bradley who—when he attended—received a payment. Sam could recall at least five calls he received from distressed residents requesting their help instead of Bradley or Olga. Such was the management problem there.

In one instance, a lady resident had a fall outside her flat and she, all seven stone of her, could not get up. A visiting carer called Bradley to help lift her. He replied, "I am not allowed to touch her. Wait for the ambulance." Typical response from Bradley jobsworth!

Sam was aware of what Bradley was saying. Sam later said, "She was a very fragile resident and obviously in a distressed state; for once, empathy would have been a better option."

On another occasion that he was on site, a resident needed to pull the emergency cord. When the medic team turned up, Bradley and his wife were turned away by the victim pleading, "Don't let them in. We want Sam and Lily." This was because previously on such a call out, management were abusive, blaming the victim for negligence regarding maintenance of a blocked shower, but when the call was made later, it was proved to be the builder's negligence, even then the resident paid nearly £200 for work done.

This was the side of Bradley residents never saw, but Sam and Lily did often. In situations like this, firstly the patient is distressed and needs empathy. Sam said it was as if the manager and his wife did not really want to be disturbed for the out-of-hours call payment.

Some residents would have never believed this comment. They always thought the sun always shone out of his proverbial ***. If you befriended Sam, you were the enemy. Bradley really was a smiling enemy and had a nasty side to him, and his wife was very similar.

Then there were the refuse bins. There was an official weekly fee for dealing with this service. The residents suspected that no one ever knew that it was legitimate but they all, well, a few of them, were aware where the money went.

Money was well spent by Bradley as the refuse room was always immaculate. Because of costs though, the fan was always switched off at the mains. Only Bradley and his wife Olga knew this. Also, the residents never knew that he was paid extra to do this. They assumed it was part of his duty. No written evidence was ever seen.

Also, every Thursday morning at 8 am, they would both drive off to her warden's post. He did the bins there and returned about half an hour later. Usually on a Friday, on the notice board was written: 'taking time back, finishing early'.

"Oh," said Sam, "Bradley's military service came into play at Orton Villas beautifully." On many occasions, Bradley would show on his office door 'on site'. We knew what that meant. Boy! He knew all about how to skive.

The smiling enemy.

Some residents may say, 'so what?' Well, the sanctimonious Sunshine Homes always claimed to be transparent. Again, here is yet another example of Bradley doing his own thing as and when he wanted, and a few strong residents looking the other way. Sam was just a troublemaker in the eyes of many residents, and that was why the community was breaking up. In some cases, residents—as previously stated—stopped talking to each other. How sad was that and there were two people given a free privileged parking space, a rent-free flat, £13,000 per year, an always rising salary and were allowed to control a £100,000 annual finance budget. The residents were never consulted, only ever told. They were trapped in their own homes, bullied, treated and controlled like seven-year-olds. After all this time of their campaign to get this couple removed, was anyone finally listening? Sam and Lily thought they were!

Again, some residents would condemn particularly Sam for all these accusations. They would even ask for proof. There is no smoke without fire. They all knew this. Let's wait and see.

A note of observation here: residents would only whisper their grievances. These two wardens had made residents too frightened to speak out.

Chapter 18

Sam's next thought was about the bingo machine. In the accounts ending November, was an entry for a donation to Bradley's local charity for the hire of a bingo machine twice. It was Bradley and his wife's favourite charity, whose premises were in Sam's town.

Sam raised this incident with Helga but got no proper reply except that the amount was raised. So why charge for it when both enjoyed so many privileges as residents at Orton Villas?

Well, would you believe what happened next? A bingo evening was arranged and naturally, residents were expecting a no-charge session when suddenly Bradley announced that the bingo machine was broken again and they would have to pay for it. The residents were unaware of the charge for the use of the machine. So sorry! Hence no bingo. Remember readers: it was Bradley borrowing and charging for the bingo machine that the residents thought was their own machine. After all this time, residents finally started to see that Bradley was being even more underhanded.

However, a little time later, a resident offered to buy another one, but before a definite decision was taken, he with Olga by his side, announced that his local charity had generously decided to offer free of charge their now repaired bingo machine. Was this a guilty gesture? So the planned replacement was put on hold. Something had happened and for a change, it worked in Orton Villas' favour.

Then suddenly, another mediation meeting was called for a second time for the three of them: Sam, Lily and Bradley to attend with naturally the two mediators also being there.

It was a typical November day. The meeting was scheduled at 2 pm. It was a very damp, rainy day, just a short drive away. Sam and Lily were in their car, Bradley in his own, alone. They arrived in a side road to find this mediation venue; it was an old pub. It looked neglected, built in the '50s perhaps. It was open, with two persons behind the bar, and two customers. When they explained why they were there, a person pointed a finger in the direction of the stairs and pointed to the upstairs.

First impression—what awful premises they had been brought to! Extremely musty smell, damp and dark; certainly, on this day, it was very unwelcoming. They entered the large and cold concert room. Sitting there in front of an extremely small electric fire and no other heat was a confident looking Bradley and two mediators, who immediately apologised for the venue. It was the best and the cheapest they could find. Bradley was dressed as if it was a summer day, Sam and Lily were dressed for the room. The impression was that it was like being in an interrogation cell during the war.

So, in a small circle of five chairs, slightly huddled, they sat. The person in charge opened the informal meeting. She apologised for the lack of suitable accommodation and no heat and explained how she would conduct the mediation. She went on to say why they were there, their differences, and that Lily would have five minutes, then Sam, and then Bradley would have a brief opportunity to recap from their first meeting and to see if they three could bond a little.

Up stood Lily, confidently, if not a little nervously. She had her say on how upset she was about having been misled on how Bradley could organise Orton Villas with no control from senior management. They never would have bought into his regime if they had known how it would turn out, then she sat down. Then the lady chairperson turned to Sam, "Would you like to continue?" she asked.

Up stood Sam. He had been to meetings before, many times, naturally. He was not trying to become over friendly with Bradley, and began asking why he was such a bully, 'always right', was not honest, why he stole the garden from them and why did he upset many residents by saying, "We have enough garden awards (five in three years). I do not want to wallpaper my walls with anymore." Sam was trembling as he spoke very emotionally.

Then would you believe it, the lady interrupted Sam to say, "Come on, we have been down this road before, we should move on."

Immediately, Sam cried out, "I knew it, this meeting is just like others. You are biased towards Bradley," and started to storm out of a now warmer room.

Firstly, the four seated were surprised, but not Bradley. He gave a little chuckle linked to a smirk. "Come back," shouted Lily.

"Please come back," implored the lady mediator, but "No!" was an adamant reply from Sam. He went down the stairs and eventually found an exit door. Cries from both ladies went unheard as he stormed out the door, still angrily shouting abuse about the 'fixed' meeting.

Now outside and back into the horrible weather, Lily caught up with Sam, and pleaded, "Please come back." Again there was an adamant, "No!" from Sam as they entered his car and drove off.

Chapter 19

Sam was not having that sort of—what he thought as—really pious attitude. *Again*, Sam thought, *who is the victim here?* Also, secretly in the distance, he began to hear now—not so faintly—the fat lady singing. Was it Orton Villas' time; was it now the beginning of the end? Only a couple of days later, Sam had two telephone calls to tell him that although a meeting between Sam and Bradley had been suggested by the mediators again, Bradley replied to say that he did not wish to proceed.

This news came as a surprise, but immediately, both Sam and Lily began talking to each other. "We shall have to wait and see," remarked Sam. What would the outcome be?

Later that week, Barbara overheard Bradley talking to a close friend saying, "It was a very damaging report and I have no choice but to accept it."

Was this what they were waiting for?

Then the truth was out. In the last few days of November, Sam received a phone call stating that Bradley was moving on. "Sacked would be nearer the truth," Sam said.

A few days later, when Sam and Lily returned from their holiday, there it was on the office door. "My wife has been offered a large promotion 30 miles away as a house warden. I (Bradley) will be leaving Orton Villas as manager and taking a part-time position there locally. I want to thank you all for your support in the past."

Sam and Lily were elated with the news. Albeit it also stated that this would be reviewed at a later date, whatever that meant! What could that mean? It was never mentioned again.

The pair of them was so lucky, why? Caring for elderly people is a vocation, a training. What training? Sam and others had always remarked that Bradley and Olga never possessed any vocation, just bullying, as these last few days had proved. So finally, 'Mr and Mrs Mannering', as they were affectionately known, had been relieved of their 'posh' home. There was no real happiness there then, despite their facial expressions. It took nearly five hundred days to reach this change but this was the news Sam and Lily had been waiting for. Sam and Lily could not disguise how they felt and their excitement showed on their smiling faces.

Both Sam and Lily never saw their regional manager again! Positive residents were loudly saying, "Well done!"

Obviously, Sam and Lily must have been heard by their regional manager, who also must be credited. Their complaints were taken seriously by him and they will never know what really happened. Therefore, they concluded that there is no smoke without a fire and most importantly, truth did finally win in the end.

As for Bradley and his wife Olga, she was very pleased with her new warden position, but poor

Bradley! Well, he certainly took a fall, not that it would bother him too seriously. Bradly would always come up smiling. He was just one of those arrogant persons who was always right, but Sam wanted to look him in the eyes and say those well-known words, "Gotcha!" This was not to be.

So, Orton Villas was to be left with a beautiful memory of their second home, their garden, totally destroyed over jealousy (not, as they claimed, Health and Safety). Shame on you, Helga, you moved them on for your convenience. Yes, out of sight, but never out of mind. It was a really dirty act. Shame on you!

Bradley once said, "You will never get me out of Orton Villas." Well, most residents were pleased when he did leave, but he not only lost a large battle but when the fat lady could be heard singing very loudly, they all knew the war was over. So now for the stories that a few residents did not want to believe—the inquest. Sam was aware that he had made some enemies, but told those who would listen, "I was always told as a child to never tell lies. If my mum thought I had, she could tell. She would say put your tongue out. Why? To this day, I do not know." All Sam was saying to a few happy residents was, "I just told the truth. It was management's decision to act as they did. We residents will never know the truth but it is true that actions speak louder than words."

There is more. Now that the truth was out, the female resident who was most upset by this happening was the lady who was Bradley's coffee maker; a very good listener to his many problems, his confidant, the lady residents whispered about in corners. (Oh yes, they did!).

Well, she told residents that she, along with another resident, believed that Bradley and Olga deserved a leaving money gift collection, which she would organise. This would be carried out by a door-to-door collection.

About one-third of residents were in favour, the rest as with all decisions at Orton Villas, went along with the idea of an open collection. Sam had residents telling him that it was no secret when the knock on the door came, the residents asked what were the others giving? Well, many felt under pressure to follow suit. A large amount of cash was collected and many gifts, making them believe that they were truly appreciated, when the majority were pleased to get rid of them. (Oh yes, they were!).

Sam recorded that the day had arrived for them both to leave—a damp and cold January day!

This was when Sam and Lily were seen to have placed their personal flags, the famous Union Flag out on their balcony to see 'Mr and Mrs Mannering' leave very quietly from a rear entrance. Sam recorded and told residents that he could see sticking out of the top of a very well-known supermarket bag the controversial bingo machine allegedly given as a goodwill gift to Orton Villas' residents by the local charity chairman Bradley. How's that for spite?

Remember residents, this allegedly was a free gift given by Bradley as a replacement.

Chapter 20

A few reflections on events at Orton Villas over five years, as remembered by Sam and Lily.

Reflections 1

Sunshine Homes! As this story unfolded, many times the pull cord or wrist or neck alarms are featured very often. Why? Because when operated after 5 pm daily and Saturday and Sunday for all of 24 hours, residents did not pay for call out; however, if the residents did use the system, someone at call line would pick up the call. This was just part of the service.

In Sam's opinion, at a cost to the house's annual budget, in the early days of his arrival, the leaseholder was allowed for a relief manager at £50 per day through the usual frugality of the local manager. The maximum allowed amount was five hours per day. Even then, management always suggested that a maximum of only £400 was required annually.

However, as previously mentioned, Bradley, despite his cut from the call-out charge, was never ever keen on such charges, because only very rarely would he be called out and many times, he was heard telling his brown envelope residents that for that sort of allowance, well, let the call-out people and the ambulance guys do it. In any case, he and his wife were not married to Sunshine Homes, they had a life. Fair enough, residents would say, but records showed and Sam had proof that many times no relief manager was available and residents would have to call the doctor or medical team in the first instance whilst waiting for the care people's system to effect itself.

Invariably, first on the scene was a resident, as stated before, no relief manager. Residents panicked and the rules went out the window. Then there was trouble because the medical team would be let in against all regulations so the locker holding the key could not be opened easily as the entry key could not be obtained. When this happened, Mr and Mrs Sunshine Homes, you have not got a clue as to how the injured and relatives reacted. Sunshine Homes does not understand empathy, only how much it will cost. If the relief manager is not there, how does he see the relatives' reactions?

Sam is about to relate to all readers a true story of events that occurred not far from Sunshine Homes.

Firstly, this retirement home had agreed to allow, under the usual local management's persuasion, one of his most popular sayings, "You don't want to go down that road," suggesting that they do not need to spend money wastefully. Under this persuasion, residents agreed to £400 annual cost towards the relief manager costs. However, the house manager announced that already £160 (then it was six months into the fiscal year) had been spent, which would leave only the balance to see the house through the autumn and winter so much care was needed to protect the budget. This sort of fear was not good for residents to hear.

So, like many residents, this very elderly but alert and mentally strong resident was alone. The management team was not breaking any rules so there was no relief manager on duty. In an emergency, this lady could pull the standard call cord. The following is what occurred.

It was just after 8 pm in the evening. The lady fell 10 feet from the pull cord and 20 feet from the door entrance. She was okay mentally, but was too weak to climb up to the sofa. She tried for half an hour to shuffle along the floor to safety but was unable to move. So half an hour later, she pulled her wrist band. There was an immediate reply, "How can we help you?" They got the lady's name so she was now reassured that help would be coming soon, or so she thought! Another 30 minutes passed by. Many reassurances were also passed on by the telephone operator.

"Why the delay?" the lady asked.

"We cannot open the main door!" came a reply.

A voice asked, "Why?"

"Aha it's open, a resident has opened the main entrance door," (this was totally forbidden). Under no circumstances must any person except the medical team touch the door. By now it was well after 9 pm. The resident had failed to move anywhere. Her only contact was still with the emergency caller, and the resident was still where she been since just after 8 pm. The main-entrance door was open. The medics now opened a special box with their standard personal code number, but there was no key to open the resident's main door. Shouts through the intercom were heard, "It must be there!"

Panicked replies were heard again through the intercom, "It's not!" This poor elderly resident was still sitting on the floor. Thank God she was not seriously injured.

She was shouting, "How can the key be missing?"

Along the corridor, voices were heard, familiar voices, "We are coming."

The two medics arrived without the important key. Through the letterbox a voice asked the lady and it was now nearly 10 pm, 120 minutes since the call was made. "Can you shuffle to the flat door?" Outside in the corridor, residents were asking where the manager was. For this reason, it would show how important a relief manager is. For this serious incident, senior management was blamed for allowing residents to agree it was too expensive, and that the annual budget would cost more than it was appropriate, anyway. That is what they had been told.

She replied, "I will try." Somebody from the other side tried to pass the key to her through the letter box.

"I cannot reach it," she cried nervously. At this point, there were now even more interested onlookers in the surrounding corridors. Outside the medic suggested another way. By now he explained he had removed his tie. He would push it through the letter box, then to tie the keys onto the tie. By now, after two hours, a very tired, frustrated and independent elderly resident was being asked to shuffle to obtain the key with which she frailly managed to connect the key and tie together. What a dreadful and disturbing experience for a 90-year-old! Seconds later, the door opened and both victim and rescuer were united. This 90-year-old was very lucky that she was conscious all through this avoidable incident. She was shaken but not very badly.

There was an ending. Early the following morning, a person was seen through the door entry camera, just visible, opening the key box and placing something in it, then closing it again. Yes, maybe a memory loss regarding the MT safe box. Someone had failed to put the key back when it was used last. On reflection, mishaps do occur, but can be avoided if empathy prevails over frugality. In this instance, Orton Villas had a lucky escape.

Was this a cover up? Although officially reported to management, there was never a proper satisfactory reply regarding these events. It may have been suggested that owing to residents' interference and opening the door against all the rules, they were in the wrong. The missing key, well that was another matter!

Relief manager's appointments should not be made by 12 head-nodders, with management persuasion but by a private vote, with more than 50% present.

To be told by the management that spending money on a service like the pull cord system is not the best way forward, "You don't want to go down that road to pay for a relief manager," says it all. The resident never received any comment from any one at Sunshine Homes except it was, "Just one of those things, and does not occur very often." The lady was never visited. She lay in her bed, very distressed for 24 hours. The company motto was, "We care for you."

Sam asked, "Who are 'we'?"

Reflections 2

The pointed finger! When ruffled, Bradley would shout loudly, get awfully vicious, and he regularly pointed his finger in anger and also suggested that Sam should watch his back. The most prominent memory Sam recalls was when he told coffee morning residents regarding the Bloom success, "I do not want to wallpaper my walls with any more awards." Also, the occasion when Bradley decided to prevent exit from the patio doors and was successful. Fortunately, residents were allowed to look through the windows at the council land type gardens now destroyed by the ban.

Reflections 3

The bingo machine, where did the portable Hoover go? Who held the keys to the wine store? Bradley was caught once in a compromising situation in the store and got away with it. The raffle was taking place one evening and a resident had given a bottle of sherry for a raffle prize. Lo and behold! It was not anywhere to be seen. When Bradley was questioned, "Sorry," he jokingly replied, "I must have mislaid it!"

Yes, sam and Lily had, like many before, had stayed in Orton Villas' guestroom a few times when looking around before buying. Guess what, here many things were missing, especially the net curtains. The guest room was stripped of many standard items. Who took Orton Villas' sunshine umbrella? Yes, these questions were asked—one of many more.

Sam, after talking to a few residents just after the garden ban earlier, reached an agreement to place on the notice board a little note about having a Garden Club. This suggested that they could, as previously, contribute to flowers and grow them in Sam's greenhouse.

Alas, when the warden returned from holiday a meeting was held: Well, well! On the warden's return, Lily was the first person to see the warden who verbally flew at her shouting loudly, "In my office now! How dare you put up such a notice on my walls without my permission?" Seconds later, Lily left crying and very upset. This was another example of 'bullying'. The notice had been torn off the wall and the brown envelopers then also complained about why they should spend more money when a few residents had already accepted the ban. Seven residents felt this way.

Obviously, no meeting took place. Most of the remaining residents, in fear of speaking, remained quiet as if they might be speaking out of turn. All that was planned was to collect £50 to provide some summer colour here at Orton Villas. As a reminder if it is needed: other developments did this nationally, but Orton Villas was prohibited from entering the garden. Remember, they were banned by the local Sunshine Homes' area manager from entering their one council-looking, neglected garden. This was a £5,000,000 development. To the management team—"Shame on you," and much more, that Sam could expound on.

Here ends my story.

My advice to the readers: think twice about retirement flats! Look behind the facade of new buildings and smiling sales people. All that glitters is not gold, as only after a long struggle and much heartache, were Sam and Lily successful.